MAGIC EYE

A New Way of Looking at the World

3D Illusions by N.E. Thing Enterprises

PENGUIN BOOKS

PENGUIN BOOKS

Published by the Penguin Group
Penguin Books Ltd, 27 Wrights Lane, London W8 5TZ, England
Penguin Books USA Inc., 375 Hudson Street, New York, New York 10014, USA
Penguin Books Australia Ltd, Ringwood, Victoria, Australia
Penguin Books Canada Ltd, 10 Alcorn Avenue, Toronto, Ontario, Canada M4V 3B2
Penguin Books (NZ) Ltd, 182–190 Wairau Road, Auckland 10, New Zealand

Penguin Books Ltd, Registered Offices: Harmondsworth, Middlesex, England

First published in Great Britain by Michael Joseph 1994
Published in Penguin Books 1995
3 5 7 9 10 8 6 4 2

Copyright © N. E. Thing Enterprises, 1994
All rights reserved

Made and printed in Great Britain by William Clowes Ltd, Beccles and London

INTRODUCTION

So, what is a MAGIC EYE picture? How does it work? Most importantly, how can you learn to "see" it too?

MAGIC EYE is the method of viewing a unique 3D picture that can be printed on plain paper with no special coatings, and viewed without special glasses. The basic idea has been around for many years. Some people call early variations of MAGIC EYE pictures Single Image Random Dot Stereograms.

During the 1960s, Dr Bella Julesz was the first to use computer-generated 3D images made up of randomly placed dots to study depth perception in human beings. In the years that followed, other people continued using random dot pictures in their work; many of them were graduate students who studied with Dr Julesz. With time they found new and better ways to create their interesting illusions.

In recent years, hobbyists and artists have advanced this amazing technique. They not only saw that further technical innovation was possible based on the basic random dot technique, but also that an entirely new art form might be possible. Powerful home computers have made both art and science based on extensive computations available to anyone who had the energy to explore these new frontiers. One notable person who has ventured into this area is Dan Dyckman, whose various entertainments and articles have enriched many of us. Another is Mike Bielinski, whose art and technical products have vastly broadened the awareness and appreciation of STARE-E-O 3D imaging.

We, at N.E. Thing Enterprises, have worked for the past years with our partner company in Japan, Tenyo Co. Ltd. In Japan, STARE-E-O images and MAGIC EYE books have skyrocketed into a major cultural phenomenon. More than 750,000 MAGIC EYE books sold there in a period of eight months, spanning 1992 and 1993; 200,000 copies were sold in Korea during the first month of publication! In addition, over a dozen competing books have been published, with many unique, beautiful, and interesting images created by a growing worldwide community of 3D artists! In Japan, 3D image viewing has been the subject of many TV talk and quiz shows.

For us, it has been a wild ride. Like many magical experiences, it soon took over those of us who naively "rubbed the lantern". So, prepare yourself. Once you discover and train your MAGIC EYE, you'll never doubt that no matter what you think you see, there's more to be revealed.

VIEWING TECHNIQUES

Learning to use your MAGIC EYE is a bit like learning to ride a bicycle. Once you get it, it gets easier and easier. If possible, try to learn to use your MAGIC EYE in a quiet, meditative time and place. It is difficult for most people to first experience deep vision while otherwise preoccupied. While others teach you, or watch as you try, you're likely to feel foolish and suffer from performance anxiety. Although MAGIC EYE is great fun at work and other entertaining social situations, those are not often the best places to learn. If you don't get it in two or three minutes, wait until another, quieter time. And, if it's hard for you, remember, the brain fairy did not skip your pillow. For most people, it's a real effort to figure out how to use the MAGIC EYE. Almost all of them tell us the effort was well worth it!

In all of the images in MAGIC EYE, you'll note a repeating pattern. In order to "see" a MAGIC EYE picture, two things must happen. First, you must get *one* eye to look at a point in the image, while the *other* eye looks at the same point in the next pattern. Second, you must hold your eyes in that position long enough for the marvellous structures in your brain to decode the 3D information that has been coded into the repeating patterns by our computer programs.

There are two methods of viewing our 3D images: Crossing your eyes and diverging your eyes. Crossing your eyes occurs when you aim your eyes at a point between your eyes and an image; diverging your eyes occurs when your eyes are aimed at a point beyond the image.

All of our pictures are designed to be seen by diverging the eyes. It is also possible to see them with the cross-eyed method, but all the depth information comes out backwards! (If you try it, we *can* guarantee that *you* will not come backwards, too.) If we intend to show an aeroplane flying in front of a cloud, using the diverging eye method, you will see an aeroplane-shaped hole cut into the cloud if you look at it with the cross-eyed method. Once you learn one method, try the other. It's fun, but most people do better with one or the other. We think that most people prefer the diverging method.

Another common occurrence is to diverge the eyes twice as far as is needed to see the image. In this case, a weird, more complex version of the intended object is seen.

One last note before you start. Although this technique is safe, and even potentially helpful to your eyes, don't overdo it! Straining will not help, and could cause you to feel uncomfortable. That is not the way to proceed. Ask your nephew or the paper girl to give you some help; they'll probably be able to do it in ten seconds. The key is to relax and let the image come to you.

METHOD ONE

Hold the image so that it touches your nose. (Ignore those who might be tempted to make comments about you.) Let the eyes relax, and stare vacantly off into space, as if looking through the image. Relax and become comfortable with the idea of observing the image, without looking *at* it. When you are relaxed and not crossing your eyes, move the page *slowly* away from your face, perhaps an inch every two or three seconds. Keep looking through the page. Stop at a comfortable reading distance and keep staring. The most discipline is needed when something starts to "come in", because at that moment you'll instinctively try to look *at* the page rather than looking through it. If you look *at* it, *start again*.

METHOD TWO

The cover of this book is shiny; hold it in such a way that you can identify a reflection. For example, hold it under an overhead lamp so that it catches its light. Simply look at the object you see reflected, and continue to stare at it with a fixed gaze. After several seconds, you'll perceive depth, followed by the 3D image, which will develop almost like an instant photo!

The images in this book are of increasing difficulty. The last pages provide a key that shows the 3D picture which you'll see when you find and train your MAGIC EYE.

The first three images in the book do not contain a hidden picture; instead the various repeated objects will seem to float in space at different distances when viewed correctly. For many, they are easier to see than the other pictures.

We wish you luck, and hope you enjoy this fantastic new art form!

24

25

Page 8 Heart

Page 9 Star

Page 10 The World

Page 11 Raindrop

Page 12 Cube

Page 13 Boxing Kangaroos

Page 14 Train

Page 15 Hot Rod

Page 16 Deer

Page 17 Aliens

Page 18 Ludwig van Beethoven

Page 19 Lamb

Page 20 Paper Stars

Page 21 Flower

Page 22 Still Life

Page 23 X29 / Fighter Plane

Page 24 Motor Bike

Page 25 Horse

Page 26 Skull

Page 27 Dolphins

Page 28–29 Dinosaurs

Page 30 Crystal Ball